The CopyWorkBook

George Washington's Rules of Civility & Decent Behavior in Company and Conversation

BLUE SKY DAISIES

Published by Blue Sky Daisies
Wichita, Kansas
blueskydaisies.wordpress.com

Cover art: George Washington, by Gilbert Stuart, 1796.

ISBN-13: 978-1-944435-02-8
ISBN-10: 1-944435-02-6

Copywork

In compiling this copybook, we have reproduced George Washington's famous *Rules of Civility and Decent Behavior in Company and Conversation*. In some instances, we have modernized spelling and conventions so that students are copying proper forms. However, we have not rewritten the rules in modern speech, just as we would not rewrite Shakespeare's language to suit our ears, but instead would endeavor to accustom our students' ears to earlier forms of English.

Copywork is useful on two fronts: first, the student has practice in developing the skill of carefully and accurately copying sentences and faithfully and neatly reproducing them; second, the student has the opportunity to set his or her mind upon excellent language and meaning.

The Editors
Blue Sky Daisies

The Rules for Civility & Decent Behavior in Company & Conversation

The collection of rules and maxims found in this copybook were discovered in a copybook kept by a young George Washington. It is likely that Washington was given the task of copying the maxims by his schoolmaster. Modern researchers believe the rules were taken from a French collection of rules attributed to the Jesuits, first seen in English in the 17th century. [1]

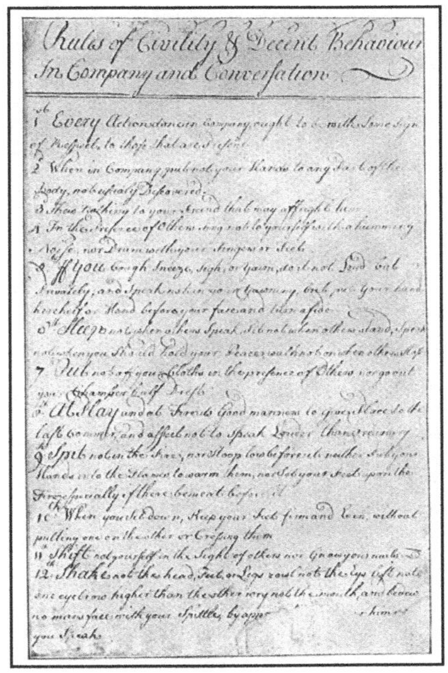
Rules of Civility & Decent Behaviour In Company and Conversation

George Washington's copy of the *Rules for Civility and Decent Behavior in Company and Conversation*. Image: *Library of Congress*

A maxim is a concise way of stating a truth or rule of conduct, and the word "maxim" comes from the Latin "maximus" for "greatest," which suggests that a maxim is a way of expressing an important truth or rule. *The Rules of Civility and Decent Behavior in Company and Conversation* has 110 maxims regarding manners and etiquette. While some of the rules may seem outmoded, the primary guiding principle of behavior is timeless: put others first.

Each rule is given a page for copywork and at the back of this book, on page 117, the entire list of rules can be seen together.

1 *http://www.foundationsmag.com/civility.html accessed January, 2017.*

1st

Every action done in company ought to be with some sign of respect to those that are present.

Copy the rule on the lines below.

Paraphrase the rule in your own words.

George Washington

2nd

When in company put not your hands to any part of the body not usually discovered.

Copy the rule on the lines below.

Paraphrase the rule in your own words.

George Washington

3rd

Show nothing to your friend that may affright him.

Affright - frighten or scare

Copy the rule on the lines below.

Paraphrase the rule in your own words.

George Washington

4th

In the presence of others, sing not to yourself with a humming noise, nor drum with your fingers or feet.

Copy the rule on the lines below.

Paraphrase the rule in your own words.

George Washington

5th

If you cough, sneeze, sigh, or yawn, do it not loud, but privately, and speak not your yawning, but put your handkerchief or hand before your face and turn aside.

Copy the rule on the lines below.

Paraphrase the rule in your own words.

George Washington

6th

Sleep not when others speak, sit not when others stand, speak not when you should hold your peace, walk not on when others stop.

Copy the rule on the lines below.

Paraphrase the rule in your own words.

George Washington

7th

Put not off your clothes in the presence of others, nor go out your chamber half dressed.

Copy the rule on the lines below.

Paraphrase the rule in your own words.

George Washington

8th

At play and at fire, it's good manners to give place to the last comer, and affect not to speak louder than ordinary.

In George Washington's day, without heated homes, it was natural to gather around the fireplace for warmth. The closest spot to the fireplace was the best spot.

Copy the rule on the lines below.

Paraphrase the rule in your own words.

George Washington

9th

Spit not in the fire, nor stoop low before it; neither put your hands into the flames to warm them, nor set your feet upon the fire, especially if there be meat before it.

The fire was a place to gather, especially in winter when the hearth offered the only heat in the home. But fires were also where the food ("meat") was cooked and prepared. Etiquette around the fire was an important part of social graces.

Copy the rule on the lines below.

Paraphrase the rule in your own words.

George Washington

10th

When you sit down, keep your feet firm and even, without putting one on the other or crossing them.

Copy the rule on the lines below.

Paraphrase the rule in your own words.

George Washington

11th

Shift not yourself in the sight of others, nor gnaw your nails.

Copy the rule on the lines below.

Paraphrase the rule in your own words.

George Washington

12th

Shake not the head, feet, or legs. Roll not the eyes, lift not one eyebrow higher than the other, wry not the mouth, and bedew no man's face with your spittle by approaching too near him when you speak.

Wry - twist
Spittle - spit
Bedew - wet or sprinkle with water or liquid

Copy the rule on the lines below.

Paraphrase the rule in your own words.

George Washington

13th

Kill no vermin as fleas, lice, ticks, etc., in the sight of others. If you see any filth or thick spittle, put your foot dexterously upon it. If it be upon the clothes of your companions, put it off privately, and if it be upon your own clothes, return thanks to him who puts it off.

In Washington's time, bathing practices were quite different from today. People rarely bathed. Hair went unwashed, bugs were everywhere, and everyone smelled. The principle of putting others first again is our guide: never embarrass others by pointing out their bugs, dirt, or spittle (spit, perhaps from tobacco) upon them.

Copy the rule on the lines below.

Paraphrase the rule in your own words.

George Washington

14th

Turn not your back to others, especially in speaking. Jog not the table or desk on which another reads or writes. Lean not upon anyone.

Copy the rule on the lines below.

Paraphrase the rule in your own words.

George Washington

15th

Keep your nails clean and short, also your hands and teeth clean, yet without showing any great concern for them.

Copy the rule on the lines below.

Paraphrase the rule in your own words.

George Washington

16th

Do not puff up the cheeks, loll not out the tongue, rub the hands or beard, thrust out the lips or bite them, or keep the lips too open or too close.

Loll - hang or droop

Copy the rule on the lines below.

Paraphrase the rule in your own words.

George Washington

17th

Be no flatterer, neither play with any that delights not to be played withal.

Copy the rule on the lines below.

Paraphrase the rule in your own words.

George Washington

18th

Read no letters, books, or papers in company, but when there is a necessity for the doing of it you must ask leave. Come not near the books or writings of another so as to read them unless desired or give your opinion of them unasked. Also look not nigh when another is writing a letter.

Copy the rule on the lines below.

Paraphrase the rule in your own words.

George Washington

19th

Let your countenance be pleasant but in serious matters somewhat grave.

Copy the rule on the lines below.

Paraphrase the rule in your own words.

George Washington

20th

The gestures of the body must be suited to the discourse you are upon.

Copy the rule on the lines below.

Paraphrase the rule in your own words.

George Washington

21st

Reproach none for the infirmities of nature, nor delight to put them that have in mind thereof.

Copy the rule on the lines below.

Paraphrase the rule in your own words.

George Washington

22nd

Show not yourself glad at the misfortune of another though he were your enemy.

Copy the rule on the lines below.

Paraphrase the rule in your own words.

George Washington

23rd

When you see a crime punished, you may be inwardly pleased; but always show pity to the suffering offender.

Copy the rule on the lines below.

Paraphrase the rule in your own words.

George Washington

24th

Do not laugh too loud or too much at any public spectacle.

Copy the rule on the lines below.

Paraphrase the rule in your own words.

George Washington

25th

Superflous complements and all affection of ceremony are to be avoided, yet where due they are not to be neglected.

Copy the rule on the lines below.

Paraphrase the rule in your own words.

George Washington

26th

In pulling off your hat to persons of distinction, as noblemen, justices, churchmen etc., make a reverence, bowing more or less according to the custom of the better bred, and quality of the person. Amongst your equals expect not always that they should begin with you first, but to pull off the hat when there is no need is affectation. In the manner of saluting and resaluting in words keep to the most usual custom.

Copy the rule on the lines below.

Paraphrase the rule in your own words.

George Washington

27th

'Tis ill manners to bid one more eminent than yourself be covered as well as not to do it to whom it's due. Likewise he that makes too much haste to put on his hat does not well, yet he ought to put it on at the first, or at most the second time of being asked; now what is herein spoken of qualification in behavior in saluting, ought also to be observed in taking of place, and sitting down for ceremonies without bounds is troublesome.

Copy the rule on the lines below.

Paraphrase the rule in your own words.

George Washington

28th

If anyone come to speak to you while you are are sitting stand up, though he be your inferior, and when you present seats let it be to every one according to his degree.

Present seats - seat your guests, i.e. chose their place in the seating arrangement

Copy the rule on the lines below.

Paraphrase the rule in your own words.

George Washington

29th

When you meet with one of greater quality than yourself, stop and retire, especially if it be at a door or any straight place to give way for him to pass.

Copy the rule on the lines below.

Paraphrase the rule in your own words.

George Washington

30th

In walking, the highest place in most countries seems to be on the right hand; therefore, place yourself on the left of him whom you desire to honor. But if three walk together, the middist place is the most honorable; the wall is usually given to the most worthy if two walk together.

Copy the rule on the lines below.

Paraphrase the rule in your own words.

George Washington

31st

If any one far surpasses others, either in age, estate, or merit, yet would give place to a meaner than himself in his own lodging or elsewhere, the one ought not to except it. So he on the other part should not use much earnestness nor offer it above once or twice.

Copy the rule on the lines below.

Paraphrase the rule in your own words.

George Washington

32nd

To one that is your equal, or not much inferior, you are to give the chief place in your lodging, and he to who 'tis offered ought at the first to refuse it but at the second to accept though not without acknowledging his own unworthiness.

Copy the rule on the lines below.

Paraphrase the rule in your own words.

George Washington

33rd

They that are in dignity or in office have in all places precedency, but whilst they are young they ought to respect those that are their equals in birth or other qualities, though they have no public charge.

Copy the rule on the lines below.

Paraphrase the rule in your own words.

George Washington

34th

It is good manners to prefer them to whom we speak before ourselves, especially if they be above us, with whom in no sort we ought to begin.

Copy the rule on the lines below.

Paraphrase the rule in your own words.

George Washington

35th

Let your discourse with men of business be short and comprehensive.

Copy the rule on the lines below.

Paraphrase the rule in your own words.

George Washington

36th

Artificers and persons of low degree ought not to use many ceremonies to lords, or others of high degree, but respect and highly honor them, and those of high degree ought to treat them with afflibility and courtesy, without arrogancy.

An artificer was a craftsman or someone who works a trade (as opposed to a land owner). Although this at first sounds aristocratic to modern American ears, we can still learn to show courtesy to those of higher and lower social class than ourselves.

Copy the rule on the lines below.

Paraphrase the rule in your own words.

George Washington

37th

In speaking to men of quality do not lean nor look them full in the face, nor approach too near them at lest keep a full pace from them.

Copy the rule on the lines below.

Paraphrase the rule in your own words.

George Washington

38th

In visiting the sick, do not presently play the physician if you be not knowing therein.

Copy the rule on the lines below.

Paraphrase the rule in your own words.

George Washington

39th

In writing or speaking, give to every person his due title according to his degree and the custom of the place.

Copy the rule on the lines below.

Paraphrase the rule in your own words.

George Washington

40th

Strive not with your superiors in argument, but always submit your judgment to others with modesty.

Copy the rule on the lines below.

Paraphrase the rule in your own words.

George Washington

41st

Undertake not to teach your equal in the art himself professes; it savors of arrogance.

Savors - Tastes

Copy the rule on the lines below.

Paraphrase the rule in your own words.

George Washington

42nd

Let thy ceremonies in courtesy be proper to the dignity of his place with whom thou converses, for it is absurd to act the same with a clown and a prince.

Copy the rule on the lines below.

Paraphrase the rule in your own words.

George Washington

43rd

Do not express joy before one sick or in pain, for that contrary passion will aggravate his misery.

Copy the rule on the lines below.

Paraphrase the rule in your own words.

George Washington

44th

When a man does all he can, though it succeeds not well, blame not him that did it.

Copy the rule on the lines below.

Paraphrase the rule in your own words.

George Washington

45th

Being to advise or reprehend any one, consider whether it ought to be in public or in private, presently or at some other time, in what terms to do it, and in reproving show no signs of cholar but do it with all sweetness and mildness.

Reprehend - reprimand
Cholar - the "choleric" temperment is irritable

Copy the rule on the lines below.

____

____

____

____

____

____

Paraphrase the rule in your own words.

____

____

____

____

____

____

George Washington

46th

Take all admonitions thankfully in what time or place soever given, but afterwards not being culpable take a time or place convenient to let him know it that gave them.

Admonitions - Correction, advice
Soever - of any kind
Culpable - guilty, responsible

Copy the rule on the lines below.

Paraphrase the rule in your own words.

George Washington

47th

Mock not nor jest at anything of importance. Break no jests that are sharp biting, and if you deliver anything witty and pleasant, abstain from laughing thereat yourself.

Thereat - on account of, at that place

Copy the rule on the lines below.

Paraphrase the rule in your own words.

George Washington

48th

Wherein you reprove another be unblameable yourself; for example is more prevalent than precepts.

Copy the rule on the lines below.

Paraphrase the rule in your own words.

George Washington

49th

Use no reproachful language against any one, neither curse nor revile.

Revile - put down or insult

Copy the rule on the lines below.

Paraphrase the rule in your own words.

George Washington

50th

Be not hasty to believe flying reports to the disparagement of any.

Copy the rule on the lines below.

Paraphrase the rule in your own words.

George Washington

51st

Wear not your clothes foul, or ripped, or dusty, but see they be brushed once everyday at least and take heed that you approach not to any uncleaness.

It was not easy to wash clothes, and in between laundering clothes were brushed clean.

Copy the rule on the lines below.

Paraphrase the rule in your own words.

George Washington

52nd

In your apparel be modest and endeavor to accomodate nature rather than to procure admiration. Keep to the fashion of your equals such as are civil and orderly with respect to times and places.

Copy the rule on the lines below.

Paraphrase the rule in your own words.

George Washington

53rd

Run not in the streets, neither go too slowly, nor with mouth open. Go not shaking your arms, kick not the earth with your feet, go not upon the toes, nor in a dancing fashion.

Copy the rule on the lines below.

Paraphrase the rule in your own words.

George Washington

54th

Play not the peacock, looking everywhere about you to see if you be well decked, if your shoes fit well, if your stockings sit neatly, and clothes handsomely.

Copy the rule on the lines below.

Paraphrase the rule in your own words.

George Washington

55th

Eat not in the streets, nor in the house, out of season.

It was considered bad etiquette to eat between mealtimes, either inside or out-of-doors.

Copy the rule on the lines below.

Paraphrase the rule in your own words.

George Washington

56th

Associate yourself with men of good quality if you esteem your own reputation; for 'tis better to be alone than in bad company.

Copy the rule on the lines below.

Paraphrase the rule in your own words.

George Washington

57th

In walking up and down in a house, only with one in company if he be greater than yourself, at the first give him the right hand and stop not till he does and be not the first that turns, and when you do turn let it be with your face towards him, if he be a man of great quality, walk not with him cheek by jowl but somewhat behind him; but yet in such a manner that he may easily speak to you.

Give him the right hand - to be on the right is the plae of honor
Jowl - the cheek around the jaw; cheek by jowl - side by side

Copy the rule on the lines below.

Paraphrase the rule in your own words.

George Washington

58th

Let your conversation be without malice or envy, for 'tis a sign of a tractable and commendable nature; and in all causes of passion, admit reason to govern.

Copy the rule on the lines below.

Paraphrase the rule in your own words.

George Washington

59th

Never express anything unbecoming, nor act against the rules moral before your inferiors.

Rules moral - rules or standards of morality

Copy the rule on the lines below.

Paraphrase the rule in your own words.

George Washington

60th

Be not immodest in urging your friends to discover a secret.

Copy the rule on the lines below.

Paraphrase the rule in your own words.

George Washington

61st

Utter not base and frivilous things amongst grave and learned men, nor very difficult questions or subjects among the ignorant, or things hard to be believed. Stuff not your discourse with sentences amongst your betters nor equals.

Copy the rule on the lines below.

Paraphrase the rule in your own words.

George Washington

62nd

Speak not of doleful things in a time of mirth or at the table; speak not of melancholy things as death and wounds, and if others mention them, change, if you can, the discourse; tell not your dreams, but to your intimate friend.

Copy the rule on the lines below.

Paraphrase the rule in your own words.

George Washington

63rd

A man ought not to value himself of his achievements or rare qualities of wit, much less of his riches, virtue, or kindred.

Wit - sharp intellect

Copy the rule on the lines below.

Paraphrase the rule in your own words.

George Washington

64th

Break not a jest where none take pleasure in mirth; laugh not aloud, nor at all without occasion; deride no man's misfortune, though there seem to be some cause.

Mirth - amusement or laughter. In other words, jesting, joking, or teasing is not always appropriate.

Copy the rule on the lines below.

Paraphrase the rule in your own words.

George Washington

65th

Speak not injurious words neither in jest nor earnest; scoff at none although they give occasion.

Copy the rule on the lines below.

Paraphrase the rule in your own words.

George Washington

66th

Be not froward, but friendly and courteous, the first to salute, hear, and answer; and be not pensive when it's a time to converse.

Froward - opposite of "toward" (e.g. to and fro); also means difficult or contrary

Copy the rule on the lines below.

Paraphrase the rule in your own words.

George Washington

67th

Detract not from others, neither be excessive in commanding.

Copy the rule on the lines below.

Paraphrase the rule in your own words.

George Washington

68th

Go not not thither, where you know not whether you shall be welcome or not. Give not advice with being asked, and when desired do it briefly.

Copy the rule on the lines below.

Paraphrase the rule in your own words.

George Washington

69th

If two contend together, take not the part of either unconstrained, and be not obstinate in your opinion, in things indifferent be of the major side.

Copy the rule on the lines below.

Paraphrase the rule in your own words.

George Washington

70th

Reprehend not the imperfections of others, for that belongs to parents, masters, and superiors.

Copy the rule on the lines below.

Paraphrase the rule in your own words.

George Washington

71st

Gaze not on the marks or blemishes of others and ask not how they came. What you may speak in secret to your friend, deliver not before others.

Copy the rule on the lines below.

Paraphrase the rule in your own words.

George Washington

72nd

Speak not in an unknown tongue in company but in your own language, and that as those of quality do, and not as the vulgar. Sublime matters treat seriously.

Copy the rule on the lines below.

Paraphrase the rule in your own words.

George Washington

73rd

Think before you speak, pronounce not imperfectly, nor bring out your words too hastily, but orderly and distinctly.

Copy the rule on the lines below.

Paraphrase the rule in your own words.

George Washington

74th

When another speaks, be attentive yourself and disturb not the audience. If any hesitate in his words, help him not nor prompt him without desired. Interrupt him not, nor answer him till his speech be ended.

Copy the rule on the lines below.

Paraphrase the rule in your own words.

George Washington

75th

In the midst of discourse ask not of what one treateth, but if you perceive any stop because of your coming, you may well intreat him gently to proceed. If a person of quality comes in while you're conversing, it's handsome to repeat what was said before.

Copy the rule on the lines below.

Paraphrase the rule in your own words.

George Washington

76th

While you are talking, point not with your finger at him of whom you discourse, nor approach too near him to whom you talk, especially to his face.

Copy the rule on the lines below.

Paraphrase the rule in your own words.

George Washington

77th

Treat with men at fit times about business and whisper not in the company of others.

Treat with - discuss or talk over
Fit times - appropriate times, in this context probably in private

Copy the rule on the lines below.

Paraphrase the rule in your own words.

George Washington

78th

Make no comparisons and if any of the company be commended for any brave act of virtue, commend not another for the same.

Copy the rule on the lines below.

Paraphrase the rule in your own words.

George Washington

79th

Be not apt to relate news if you know not the truth thereof. In discoursing of things you have heard, name not your author. Always a secret discover not.

Copy the rule on the lines below.

Paraphrase the rule in your own words.

George Washington

80th

Be not tedious in discourse or in reading unless you find the company pleased therewith.

Copy the rule on the lines below.

Paraphrase the rule in your own words.

George Washington

81st

Be not curious to know the affairs of others, neither approach those that speak in private.

Copy the rule on the lines below.

Paraphrase the rule in your own words.

George Washington

82nd

Undertake not what you cannot perform but be careful to keep your promise.

Copy the rule on the lines below.

Paraphrase the rule in your own words.

George Washington

83rd

When you deliver a matter do it without passion and with discretion, however mean a person be you do it too.

A "mean" person is one who is of lower class, position, or importance; it does not suggest someone who is unkind.

Copy the rule on the lines below.

Paraphrase the rule in your own words.

George Washington

84th

When your superiors talk to anybody, hearken not, neither speak nor laugh.

Talk to anybody - correct, chastise, or reprehend (in this context)
Hearken - listen

Copy the rule on the lines below.

Paraphrase the rule in your own words.

George Washington

85th

In company of these of higher quality than yourself, speak not till you are asked a question, then stand upright, put off your hat, and answer in few words.

Copy the rule on the lines below.

Paraphrase the rule in your own words.

George Washington

86th

In disputes, be not so desirous to overcome as not to give liberty to each one to deliver his opinion, and submit to the judgment of a major part, especially if they are judges of the dispute.

Copy the rule on the lines below.

Paraphrase the rule in your own words.

George Washington

89th

Let thy carriage be such as becomes a man: grave, settled, and attentive to that which is spoken. Contradict not at every turn what others say.

Copy the rule on the lines below.

Paraphrase the rule in your own words.

George Washington

88th

Be not tedious in discourse, make not many digressions, nor repeat often the same manner of discourse.

Copy the rule on the lines below.

Paraphrase the rule in your own words.

89th

Speak not evil of the absent, for it is unjust.

Copy the rule on the lines below.

Paraphrase the rule in your own words.

George Washington

90th

Being set at meat, scratch not, neither spit, cough, or blow your nose except there's a necessity for it.

Copy the rule on the lines below.

Paraphrase the rule in your own words.

George Washington

91st

Make no show of taking great delight in your victuals. Feed not with greediness, cut your bread with a knife, lean not on the table, neither find fault with what you eat.

Copy the rule on the lines below.

Paraphrase the rule in your own words.

George Washington

92nd

Take no salt nor cut bread with your knife greasy.

Copy the rule on the lines below.

Paraphrase the rule in your own words.

George Washington

93rd

Entertaining any one at table, it is decent to present him with meat. Undertake not to help others undesired by the master.

Copy the rule on the lines below.

Paraphrase the rule in your own words.

George Washington

94th

If you soak bread in the sauce, let it be no more than what you put in your mouth at a time, and blow not your broth at table, but stay till cools off itself.

Copy the rule on the lines below.

Paraphrase the rule in your own words.

George Washington

95th

Put not your meat to your mouth with your knife in your hand, neither spit forth the stones of any fruit pie upon a dish, nor cast anything under the table.

The "stones" in a fruit pie are the pits of fruit, such as cherry pits.

Copy the rule on the lines below.

Paraphrase the rule in your own words.

George Washington

96th

It's unbecoming to stoop much to one's meat. Keep your fingers clean and when foul wipe them on a corner of your table napkin.

Copy the rule on the lines below.

Paraphrase the rule in your own words.

George Washington

97th

Put not another bite into your mouth till the former be swallowed, let not your morsels be too big for the jowls.

Copy the rule on the lines below.

Paraphrase the rule in your own words.

George Washington

98th

Drink not nor talk with your mouthful; neither gaze about you while you are a drinking.

Copy the rule on the lines below.

Paraphrase the rule in your own words.

George Washington

99th

Drink not too leisurely nor yet too hastily. Before and after drinking wipe your lips. Breath not then or ever with too great a noise, for it's uncivil.

Copy the rule on the lines below.

Paraphrase the rule in your own words.

George Washington

100th

Cleanse not your teeth with the tablecloth, napkin, fork or knife, but if others do it, let it be done with a pick tooth.

Copy the rule on the lines below.

Paraphrase the rule in your own words.

George Washington

101st

Rinse not your mouth in the presence of others.

Copy the rule on the lines below.

Paraphrase the rule in your own words.

George Washington

102nd

It is out of use to call upon the company often to eat, nor need you drink to others every time you drink.

Copy the rule on the lines below.

Paraphrase the rule in your own words.

George Washington

103rd

In the company of your betters, be not longer in eating than they are. Lay not your arm but only your hand upon the table.

Copy the rule on the lines below.

Paraphrase the rule in your own words.

George Washington

104th

It belongs to the chiefest in company to unfold his napkin and fall to meat first, But he ought then to begin in time and to dispatch with dexterity that the slowest may have time allowed him.

Copy the rule on the lines below.

Paraphrase the rule in your own words.

George Washington

105th

Be not angry at table, whatever happens, and if you have reason to be so, show it not but on a cheerful countenance, especially if there be strangers, for good humor makes one dish of meat a feast.

Copy the rule on the lines below.

Paraphrase the rule in your own words.

George Washington

106th

Set not yourself at the upper of the table; but if it be your due or that the master of the house will have it so, contend not, least you should trouble the company.

Copy the rule on the lines below.

Paraphrase the rule in your own words.

George Washington

107th

If others talk at table be attentive, but talk not with meat in your mouth.

Copy the rule on the lines below.

Paraphrase the rule in your own words.

George Washington

108th

When you speak of God or his attributes, let it be seriously and with reverence. Honor and obey your natural parents although they be poor.

Copy the rule on the lines below.

Paraphrase the rule in your own words.

George Washington

109th

Let your recreations be manful not sinful.

Copy the rule on the lines below.

Paraphrase the rule in your own words.

George Washington

110th

Labor to keep alive in your breast that little spark of celestial fire called conscience.

Copy the rule on the lines below.

Paraphrase the rule in your own words.

George Washington

The Rules of Civility & Decent Behavior in Company & Conversation

1. Every action done in company ought to be with some sign of respect to those that are present.

2. When in company put not your hands to any part of the body not usually discovered.

3. Show nothing to your friend that may affright him.

4. In the presence of others, sing not to yourself with a humming noise, nor drum with your fingers or feet.

5. If you cough, sneeze, sigh, or yawn, do it not loud, but privately, and speak not your yawning, but put your handkerchief or hand before your face and turn aside.

6. Sleep not when others speak, sit not when others stand, speak not when you should hold your peace, walk not on when others stop.

7. Put not off your clothes in the presence of others, nor go out your chamber half dressed.

8. At play and at fire, it's good manners to give place to the last comer, and affect not to speak louder than ordinary.

9. Spit not in the fire, nor stoop low before it; neither put your hands into the flames to warm them, nor set your feet upon the fire, especially if there be meat before it.

10. When you sit down, keep your feet firm and even, without putting one on the other or crossing them.

11. Shift not yourself in the sight of others, nor gnaw your nails.

George Washington

12. Shake not the head, feet, or legs. Roll not the eyes, lift not one eyebrow higher than the other, wry not the mouth, and bedew no man's face with your spittle by approaching too near him when you speak.

13. Kill no vermin as fleas, lice, ticks, etc., in the sight of others. If you see any filth or thick spittle, put your foot dexterously upon it. If it be upon the clothes of your companions, put it off privately, and if it be upon your own clothes, return thanks to him who puts it off.

14. Turn not your back to others, especially in speaking. Jog not the table or desk on which another reads or writes. Lean not upon anyone.

15. Keep your nails clean and short, also your hands and teeth clean, yet without showing any great concern for them.

16. Do not puff up the cheeks, loll not out the tongue, rub the hands or beard, thrust out the lips or bite them, or keep the lips too open or too close.

17. Be no flatterer, neither play with any that delights not to be played withal.

18. Read no letters, books, or papers in company, but when there is a necessity for the doing of it you must ask leave. Come not near the books or writings of another so as to read them unless desired or give your opinion of them unasked. Also look not nigh when another is writing a letter.

19. Let your countenance be pleasant but in serious matters somewhat grave.

20. The gestures of the body must be suited to the discourse you are upon.

21. Reproach none for the infirmities of nature, nor delight to put them that have in mind thereof.

22. Show not yourself glad at the misfortune of another though he were your enemy.

23. When you see a crime punished, you may be inwardly pleased; but always show pity to the suffering offender.

24. Do not laugh too loud or too much at any public spectacle.

25. Superflous complements and all affection of ceremony are to be avoided, yet where due they are not to be neglected.

George Washington

26. In pulling off your hat to persons of distinction, as noblemen, justices, churchmen etc., make a reverence, bowing more or less according to the custom of the better bred, and quality of the person. Amongst your equals expect not always that they should begin with you first, but to pull off the hat when there is no need is affectation. In the manner of saluting and resaluting in words keep to the most usual custom.

27. 'Tis ill manners to bid one more eminent than yourself be covered as well as not to do it to whom it's due. Likewise he that makes too much haste to put on his hat does not well, yet he ought to put it on at the first, or at most the second time of being asked; now what is herein spoken of qualification in behavior in saluting, ought also to be observed in taking of place, and sitting down for ceremonies without bounds is troublesome.

28. If anyone come to speak to you while you are are sitting stand up, though he be your inferior, and when you present seats let it be to every one according to his degree.

29. When you meet with one of greater quality than yourself, stop and retire, especially if it be at a door or any straight place to give way for him to pass.

30. In walking, the highest place in most countries seems to be on the right hand; therefore place yourself on the left of him whom you desire to honor. But if three walk together, the middist place is the most honorable; the wall is usually given to the most worthy if two walk together.

31. If any one far surpasses others, either in age, estate, or merit, yet would give place to a meaner than himself in his own lodging or elsewhere, the one ought not to except it. So he on the other part should not use much earnestness nor offer it above once or twice.

32. To one that is your equal, or not much inferior, you are to give the chief place in your lodging, and he to who 'tis offered ought at the first to refuse it but at the second to accept though not without acknowledging his own unworthiness.

33. They that are in dignity or in office have in all places precedency, but whilst they are young they ought to respect those that are their equals in birth or other qualities, though they have no public charge.

34. It is good manners to prefer them to whom we speak before ourselves, especially if they be above us, with whom in no sort we ought to begin.

35. Let your discourse with men of business be short and comprehensive.

36. Artificers and persons of low degree ought not to use many ceremonies to lords, or others of high degree, but respect and highly honor them, and those of high degree ought to treat them with afflibility and courtesy, without arrogancy.

37. In speaking to men of quality do not lean nor look them full in the face, nor approach too near them at lest keep a full pace from them.

38. In visiting the sick, do not presently play the physician if you be not knowing therein.

39. In writing or speaking, give to every person his due title according to his degree and the custom of the place.

40. Strive not with your superiors in argument, but always submit your judgment to others with modesty.

41. Undertake not to teach your equal in the art himself professes; it savors of arrogance.

42. Let thy ceremonies in courtesy be proper to the dignity of his place with whom thou converses, for it is absurd to act the same with a clown and a prince.

43. Do not express joy before one sick or in pain, for that contrary passion will aggravate his misery.

44. When a man does all he can, though it succeeds not well, blame not him that did it.

45. Being to advise or reprehend any one, consider whether it ought to be in public or in private, presently or at some other time, in what terms to do it, and in reproving show no signs of cholar but do it with all sweetness and mildness.

46. Take all admonitions thankfully in what time or place soever given, but afterwards not being culpable take a time or place convenient to let him know it that gave them.

47. Mock not nor jest at anything of importance. Break no jest that are sharp biting, and if you deliver anything witty and pleasant, abtain from laughing thereat yourself.

48. Wherein you reprove another be unblameable yourself; for example is more prevalent than precepts.

49. Use no reproachful language against any one, neither curse nor revile.

50. Be not hasty to believe flying reports to the disparagement of any.

51. Wear not your clothes foul, or ripped, or dusty, but see they be brushed once everyday at least and take heed that you approach not to any uncleaness.

52. In your apparel be modest and endeavor to accomodate nature rather than to procure admiration. Keep to the fashion of your equals such as are civil and orderly with respect to times and places.

53. Run not in the streets, neither go too slowly, nor with mouth open. Go not shaking your arms, kick not the earth with your feet, go not upon the toes, nor in a dancing fashion.

54. Play not the peacock, looking everywhere about you to see if you be well decked, if your shoes fit well, if your stockings sit neatly, and clothes handsomely.

55. Eat not in the streets, nor in the house, out of season.

56. Associate yourself with men of good quality if you esteem your own reputation; for 'tis better to be alone than in bad company.

57. In walking up and down in a house, only with one in company if he be greater than yourself, at the first give him the right hand and stop not till he does and be not the first that turns, and when you do turn let it be with your face towards him, if he be a man of great quality, walk not with him cheek by jowl but somewhat behind him; but yet in such a manner that he may easily speak to you.

58. Let your conversation be without malice or envy, for 'tis a sign of a tractable and commendable nature; and in all causes of passion, admit reason to govern.

59. Never express anything unbecoming, nor act against the rules moral before your inferiors.

60. Be not immodest in urging your friends to discover a secret.

61. Utter not base and frivilous things amongst grave and learned men, nor very difficult questions or subjects among the ignorant, or things hard to be believed. Stuff not your discourse with sentences amongst your betters nor equals.

62. Speak not of doleful things in a time of mirth or at the table; speak not of melancholy things as death and wounds, and if others mention them, change, if you can, the discourse; tell not your dreams, but to your intimate friend.

63. A man ought not to value himself of his achievements or rare qualities of wit, much less of his riches, virtue, or kindred.

64. Break not a jest where none take pleasure in mirth; laugh not aloud, nor at all without occasion; deride no man's misfortune, though there seem to be some cause.

65. Speak not injurious words neither in jest nor earnest; scoff at none although they give occasion.

66. Be not froward, but friendly and courteous, the first to salute, hear, and answer; and be not pensive when it's a time to converse.

67. Detract not from others, neither be excessive in commanding.

68. Go not not thither, where you know not whether you shall be welcome or not. Give not advice with being asked, and when desired do it briefly.

69. If two contend together, take not the part of either unconstrained, and be not obstinate in your opinion, in things indifferent be of the major side.

70. Reprehend not the imperfections of others, for that belongs to parents, masters, and superiors.

71. Gaze not on the marks or blemishes of others and ask not how they came. What you may speak in secret to your friend, deliver not before others.

72. Speak not in an unknown tongue in company but in your own language, and that as those of quality do, and not as the vulgar. Sublime matters treat seriously.

George Washington

73. Think before you speak, pronounce not imperfectly, nor bring out your words too hastily, but orderly and distinctly.

74. When another speaks, be attentive yourself and disturb not the audience. If any hesitate in his words, help him not nor prompt him without desired. Interrupt him not, nor answer him till his speech be ended.

75. In the midst of discourse ask not of what one treateth, but if you perceive any stop because of your coming, you may well intreat him gently to proceed. If a person of quality comes in while you're conversing, it's handsome to repeat what was said before.

76. While you are talking, point not with your finger at him of whom you discourse, nor approach too near him to whom you talk, especially to his face.

77. Treat with men at fit times about business and whisper not in the company of others.

78. Make no comparisons and if any of the company be commended for any brave act of virtue, commend not another for the same.

79. Be not apt to relate news if you know not the truth thereof. In discoursing of things you have heard, name not your author. Always a secret discover not.

80. Be not tedious in discourse or in reading unless you find the company pleased therewith.

81. Be not curious to know the affairs of others, neither approach those that speak in private.

82. Undertake not what you cannot perform but be careful to keep your promise.

83. When you deliver a matter do it without passion and with discretion, however mean a person be you do it too.

84. When your superiors talk to anybody, hearken not, neither speak nor laugh.

85. In company of these of higher quality than yourself, speak not till you are asked a question, then stand upright, put off your hat, and answer in few words.

86. In disputes, be not so desirous to overcome as not to give liberty to each one to deliver his opinion, and submit to the judgment of a major part, especially if they are judges of the dispute.

87. Let thy carriage be such as becomes a man: grave, settled, and attentive to that which is spoken. Contradict not at every turn what others say.

88. Be not tedious in discourse, make not many digressions, nor repeat often the same manner of discourse.

89. Speak not evil of the absent, for it is unjust.

90. Being set at meat, scratch not, neither spit, cough, or blow your nose except there's a necessity for it.

91. Make no show of taking great delight in your victuals. Feed not with greediness, cut your bread with a knife, lean not on the table, neither find fault with what you eat.

92. Take no salt nor cut bread with your knife greasy.

93. Entertaining any one at table, it is decent to present him with meat. Undertake not to help others undesired by the master.

94. If you soak bread in the sauce, let it be no more than what you put in your mouth at a time, and blow not your broth at table, but stay till cools off itself.

95. Put not your meat to your mouth with your knife in your hand, neither spit forth the stones of any fruit pie upon a dish, nor cast anything under the table.

96. It's unbecoming to stoop much to one's meat. Keep your fingers clean and when foul wipe them on a corner of your table napkin.

97. Put not another bite into your mouth till the former be swallowed, let not your morsels be too big for the jowls.

98. Drink not nor talk with your mouthful; neither gaze about you while you are a drinking.

99. Drink not too leisurely nor yet too hastily. Before and after drinking wipe your lips. Breath not then or ever with too great a noise, for it's uncivil.

100. Cleanse not your teeth with the tablecloth, napkin, fork or knife, but if others do it, let it be done with a pick tooth.

101. Rinse not your mouth in the presence of others.

102. It is out of use to call upon the company often to eat, nor need you drink to others every time you drink.

103. In the company of your betters, be not longer in eating than they are. Lay not your arm but only your hand upon the table.

104. It belongs to the chiefest in company to unfold his napkin and fall to meat first, But he ought then to begin in time and to dispatch with dexterity that the slowest may have time allowed him.

105. Be not angry at table, whatever happens, and if you have reason to be so, show it not but on a cheerful countenance, especially if there be strangers, for good humor makes one dish of meat a feast.

106. Set not yourself at the upper of the table; but if it be your due or that the master of the house will have it so, contend not, least you should trouble the company.

107. If others talk at table be attentive, but talk not with meat in your mouth.

108. When you speak of God or his attributes, let it be seriously and with reverence. Honor and obey your natural parents although they be poor.

109. Let your recreations be manful not sinful.

110. Labor to keep alive in your breast that little spark of celestial fire called conscience.

Made in the USA
Middletown, DE
10 October 2026

34531579R00073